PLAY TENNIS

A practical step-by-step guide with Derek Horwood

The author would like to thank:

Philip Gilderdale for his help in designing this book
Jon Gray for photography
Paul Cemmick for the cartoons
Hugh Ribbans for the diagrams
Tim Shackleton and Peter Ramsden for editorial help
Dennis Van der Meer for his inspiration

Published to accompany a series of programmes
prepared in consultation with the BBC Continuing Education Advisory Council

This book accompanies the BBC Television series *Play Tennis*
first broadcast on BBC2 from 11 May 1981
Producer Peter Ramsden
Presented and demonstrated by Derek Horwood

© The Author 1981
First published 1981
Published by the British Broadcasting Corporation
35 Marylebone High Street, London W1M 4AA

ISBN 0 563 16455 7

Printed in England by
BAS Printers Limited, Over Wallop, Stockbridge, Hampshire
and bound by Hunter and Foulis Limited, Edinburgh, Scotland
This book is set in 10 on 11 point Plantin Monophoto

Many coaches would agree that tennis is a far more difficult game for beginners to learn than any of the other racket sports. For a start, a tennis racket is considerably larger and heavier than the ones used in squash or badminton, and this makes it much more difficult for a beginner to keep control over it. The court is larger, too, and again a greater amount of control is necessary in achieving consistent accuracy in your shots. Factors such as these mean that making progress in learning the basics of the game can sometimes be slower than you'd like. This is why many beginners have a tendency to rush ahead and try to do too much too soon, with the result that things are soon out of control.

The most important aspect of the method I outline in this book is that it is intended to give you that control over everything you do right from the very start. Nothing is rushed: the main principle is to slow the ball and racket movements down, so that you have time to build up and play your strokes. In the beginning this method is not competitive; indeed, I think you can only be truly competitive, when you've got the basics sorted out. When you come to play a game, you won't have time to think about how your strokes are produced – you'll be thinking about tactics, about what your opponent is doing, about what you will do next. You can only do this effectively if you have a solid grasp of the fundamentals of tennis.

You will progress better – and certainly have more fun – if there are two of you learning tennis together. This is not just because many of the exercises require the assistance of a second person, but also because you'll be able to keep an eye on each other's progress. At the start, you won't need to practice on a tennis court. Any flat, open space will do just as well, provided it has sufficient space for you to play the ball to each other.

Though I have had the beginner's interest very much at heart in the way this book is set out, I am sure it will be of value to others. Coaches and teachers with large groups of beginners, will find much of interest in this method which will enable them to teach tennis to others more successfully. Even more experienced players occasionally need a refresher course, and they too will find in these pages ways of improving aspects of their game. Above all, I hope that this book will get you off to a good start and that you'll find it both enjoyable and beneficial.

HOW TO USE THE BOOK

The aim of this book is to teach you the five basic tennis strokes in an enjoyable and positive way. The strokes are built up in ten easy steps, in a progressive, cumulative manner. I suggest that you work through the book in the order in which it has been written. You will find that four of the strokes are actually learned together; only one, the service, is treated separately.

The photographs often show both front and side views in order to demonstrate, for instance, how far in front or to the side you make contact with the ball. Dotted lines and arrows show the flight of the ball or the movement of the racket. All the illustrations show right-handed players.

The five basic strokes are shown on pages 6–13. In them, I demonstrate what I consider to be the most important aspects of each shot, so you can see at a glance their main characteristics and elements. I don't ask the beginner to attempt the entire stroke from the start, and then correct the inevitable mistakes. Each stroke is built up from first principles in ten separate steps.

Step 1, **Tossing the ball**, shows you how to set up the ball for each other to play, and how to learn the specific point at which, (when you come to use a racket) you will make contact with the ball. It will give you a feel for the rhythm and speed of the bouncing ball. This step is important because, in the steps that follow, you and your partner will need to toss the ball to each other accurately. Tossing the ball to each other in this way, will help develop your judgement and anticipation.

Step 2, **Holding the racket**, gets you used to the feel of a racket in your hand. The grip I show here isn't the one you'd use in a game of tennis – I will come to that later – but it's a very useful way of overcoming the problem of how heavy and unwieldy a racket often feels at first. It will also give you a feeling for the ball through the strings of the racket.

Step 3, **Making contact**, shows you the importance of getting the right point of contact with the ball. By using the simple grip and making a very simple stroke, everything else is eliminated and you will be able to concentrate on control and returning the ball accurately to each other.

HOW TO USE THE BOOK

Step 4, **Holding the racket**, moves on to a more advanced grip. Again, this isn't the way you'd hold the racket in a game but it is an easy way of showing you how to build up your strokes while maintaining control.

Step 5, **The follow through**, shows you how you guide the ball back to your partner after making contact. This will eventually give you more control over both the direction and pace of your shots.

Step 6, **Holding the racket**, shows you how you would normally hold the racket during a game. It demonstrates some simpler ways of finding the basic orthodox grips.

Step 7, **The backswing**, will give your ground-strokes more of a flowing, swinging action. The volleys do not have a great deal of backswing but they should not be neglected.

Step 8, **Are you ready?**, shows you the way to stand when you're waiting to receive the ball between shots. This will enable you to move off easily no matter what direction the ball may come from, ready to play any of the strokes you've learned.

Step 9, **Footwork**, will increase your mobility. The way you move your feet quickly into position is crucial to the way you play your shots and is essential to good tennis. You will find that footwork will come naturally with practice, enabling you to play difficult balls more easily.

Step 10, **The service**, demonstrates the most important shot in the game. This is dealt with separately, not because it's any more difficult but because although the method is the same the procedure is slightly different.

These are the ten stages through which you will learn the basics of tennis. When you feel confident enough, you can move on to The Drills (pages 84–89). These will give you practice in playing sequences of shots similar to those you'd come across during an actual game, but with the emphasis, as ever, on control rather than on winning the point. At the end of the book you'll find diagrams of the court and of the various parts of the racket, with which you will need to be familiar (page 94). There is also a simplified version of the rules of tennis and an index, which will help you refer back quickly to all the major points covered in the book.

THE FOREHAND

Ready Position   Shoulder Turn   Backswing

Forward Step   Making Contact   Follow Through

THE BACKHAND

Ready Position   Shoulder Turn   Backswing

Forward Step   Making Contact   Follow Through

THE FOREHAND VOLLEY SEQUENCE

Ready Position   Shoulder Turn   Making Contact

Ready Position   Shoulder Turn   Making Contact

Ready Position   Rhythm and Harmony   Backswing

Contact Point   Follow Through   Final Position

TOSSING THE BALL

Often a beginner doesn't have enough control to hit the ball with sufficient precision for his partner to return it. So, to start with, set the ball up for your partner by simply tossing the ball to him underarm. If you hold the ball in your fingertips with the palm uppermost, you'll be able to release the ball easily and keep maximum control of it.

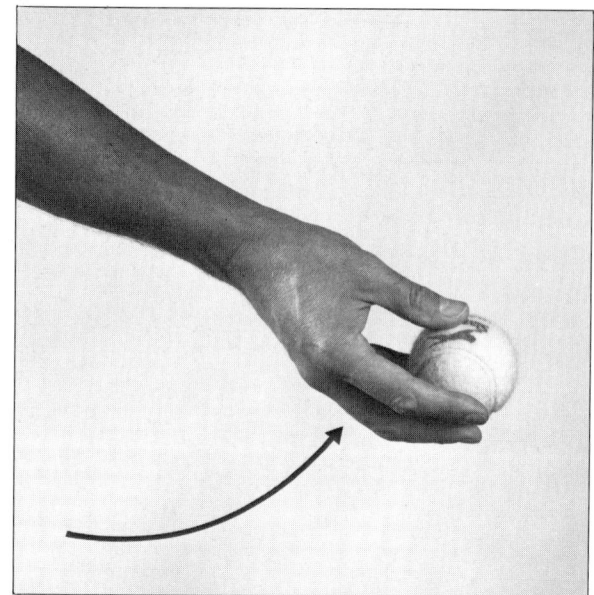

Your partner should catch the ball with his right hand, keeping his forearm outside and in front of his right leg. Tossing the ball between you and catching it in this position will give both of you a feeling for the timing and rhythm of a bouncing ball, which will help you later when you first start to use a racket.

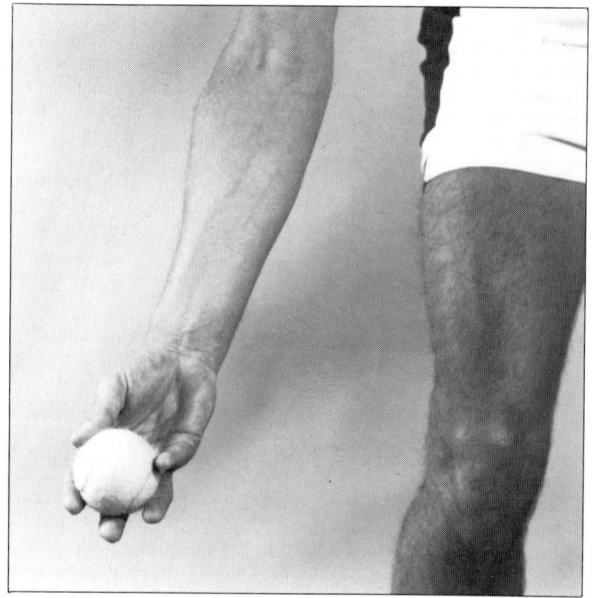

BY HAND

Toss the ball in a high arc so it bounces in front of your partner. Use a paper disc on the floor to mark the spot where the ball is going to bounce. Your partner should catch the ball just after it has reached the top of its bounce.

You should stand square on to each other with your feet shoulder width apart and the knees slightly bent. This is called 'the open stance'. Both of you should retain this position throughout this exercise.

Retaining the open stance, stand square on to each other with your throwing and catching arms opposite one another. Toss the ball to your partner so he doesn't have to move to catch it.

The aim of this exercise is to get you to set the ball up in the right place for your partner. How well he will be able to play his strokes using the racket will depend on the accuracy with which you can toss the ball for him. Once you have achieved consistent accuracy, toss the ball deliberately to the left or right so your partner has to move to catch it correctly.

Once you have mastered setting the ball up for each other, start using a racket. There are many ways of holding a racket. If you hold it with the racket head facing down, this is called a closed racket face. This will cause the ball, when you play it with a simple, flat stroke, to move downwards from the point at which it makes contact with the racket.

The racket can also be held facing upwards. This is called an open racket face. When hit flat, the ball will move upwards from the point of contact. In all the shots in this book, the ball will be hit flat and played with an open racket face.

RACKET ANGLES

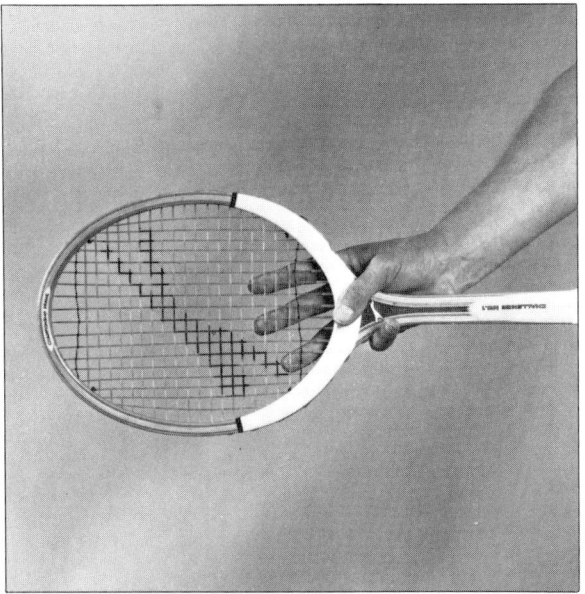

When you first hold a tennis racket, it might seem very heavy and unwieldy to you, and you probably won't be able to control it very easily. So to start with I'd recommend that you hold the racket in what I call the 'short grip'. The three middle fingers are behind the strings, the thumb and little finger around the throat of the racket.

The short grip gives you control over the racket head, and is very useful in giving you the feeling of making contact with the ball through the strings of the racket.

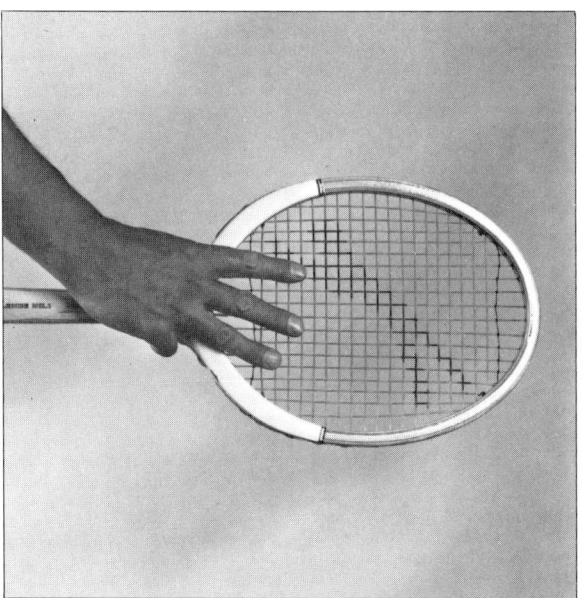

With the short grip, you hold the racket in the same way for both the forehand and backhand. On the backhand, however, your racket arm comes across in front of your body, so that the middle fingers are on the front side of your racket (the side with which you make contact with the ball), and the thumb and forefinger are around the throat on the back of the racket.

SHORT GRIP

MAKING CONTACT

Having got the feel of the short grip, face your partner in an open stance ready to play a forehand shot. Hold the racket outside and in front of your right leg, with its shaft parallel to the ground with an open racket face.

Your partner can now toss the ball to you, just as he did in the throwing and catching exercises in Step One.

Watch the movement of the ball very closely as it comes towards you, and follow it right on to the racket. Still holding your racket with an open face, flex your knees as you make contact with the ball, just after it's reached the top of its bounce. This will help give you a feeling of lifting the ball as you play it, more upwards than forwards, in a high arc to bounce back in front of your partner.

Don't at this stage, play a sweeping stroke: simply bump the ball back.

SHORT GRIP

To play the backhand, your right arm passes in front of your body, so that you're holding the shaft of the racket parallel to the ground, outside and in front of your left leg. Keep the short grip, so your three middle fingers will be on the front of the racket strings, and your thumb and little finger are around the back of the throat, providing a pushing movement towards the ball.

Once again, the racket is angled upwards with an open face. This allows the ball to be hit upwards. Follow the ball carefully, and make contact with it just after the top of the bounce.

To put movement into these shots, your partner can toss the ball left or right, long or short. Maintaining the open stance, move into position with short dance-like steps, so you can still make contact with the ball shortly after the top of the bounce, and outside and in front of your leg.

19

To play a volley you have to make contact with the ball before it bounces. All the shots you have played so far have been what are called ground strokes, where you hit the ball after it has bounced. To volley, hold the racket head at eye level, outside and in front of your right shoulder, with the shaft pointing downwards.

Your partner uses the face of the racket as a target, and tosses the ball directly on to the strings. To make contact, push the palm of the hand holding the racket at the ball.

The racket face should be open, so you can play the ball back to bounce in front of your partner. Angle your wrist so that the racket face remains open the whole time, and hold your wrist very firm. Keep your knees bent. If the ball comes to you lower than you expect, keep the racket at eye level, and bend your knees further to bring the racket down to the point where it will make contact with the ball.

SHORT GRIP

To play the backhand volley, bring the racket outside and in front of your left shoulder. As before, your partner tosses the ball directly at the racket, only this time the feeling is of pushing at the ball with the back of your hand, rather than the palm.

On the backhand volley, your fingers will be on the front of the racket, while the thumb and little finger support the back. Keep the shaft pointing to the ground, and the racket head at eye level. Keep the racket face open.

Remember to maintain your open stance and keep your knees flexed, so you can adjust easily to the height of the ball.

SHORT GRIP

Now you should be ready to play the ball back and forth with your partner, using the strokes you have learned so far. This is called a rally.

To start the first rally, you'll have to set the ball up to hit to your partner. Hold your racket parallel to the ground in the contact position, with your left hand holding the ball in front of the strings. Keep your palm up, and hold the ball in your fingertips for easy release and maximum control.

Now toss the ball up, so that it will bounce in front of you to approximately thigh height. Make contact just after it has reached the top of the bounce.

INTRODUCING THE BALL

To set the ball up for the backhand, your left hand will have to come over the top of the racket. Remember to hold the ball in your fingertips, and keep your palm facing upwards.

Once again toss the ball up, so it will bounce enabling you to make contact between knee and hip height.

Whether you play a forehand or a backhand to start your first rally, it's very important that you control the ball, so that you don't make your partner struggle to reach it. Play it quite gently so that it bounces in front of him, just as though you were tossing the ball to him. This will make it easier for him to return the ball to you.

In these first forehand-to-forehand rallies it is important to keep the pace slow, and to play the ball upwards over the net, so your partner has plenty of time to position himself for the return. Don't try to rush things at first.

Use markers on the floor to give you something to aim for.

You can also play backhand-to-backhand rallies. The longer you can keep a rally going, the more practice you will get. Don't let it become wild: by keeping things under firm control, you will not only have more opportunity to perfect your shots, but you will also acquire the discipline that is essential to good tennis. Don't try using a variety of shots in a rally. Concentrate on one shot at a time, and if you start with the backhand, move your feet around so you can continue playing it, even though the ball doesn't come to you exactly where you'd want it. If necessary, stop the rally rather than change shots.

SHORT GRIP

It isn't necessary for both of you to play the same shot in a rally: you can use different combinations. If you want to try out your volley, for instance, your partner can practise his forehand at the same time. You should play the ball so that it bounces in front of him, making it easier for him to return it directly on to your racket.

Another combination would be for you to rally with a backhand volley, while your partner plays a backhand. Remember that you should stand with your racket heads opposite one another.

Long rallies played slowly over short distances, with both players standing quite close to the net, will give you a lot of practice. As you improve your control, you can move further apart, but it's vital that you are ready to do this.

As your skills improve and you acquire greater control, you will be able to increase the rallying distance between you. When both of you feel sure that the short grip has served its purpose, you can move on to the middle grip.

To find the forehand middle grip, start by holding the racket in the short grip. Then slide your right hand down the shaft, keeping the palm in contact with the same flat surface, until you can close your fingers with the heel of your hand just touching the grip.

MIDDLE GRIP

For the backhand, hold the racket in the forehand middle grip, and pull it across the front of your body with your left hand. You'll find that there's a slight hump on your right wrist, because your palm is still in contact with the front (facing) side of the shaft.

This hump will flatten out if you turn your hand so that the palm is in contact with the top edge of the shaft. The heel of your hand will just be on the grip. This is the basis of the backhand grip, though there are refinements which I'll cover when you come to the full grip.

MIDDLE GRIP

Once you've got the feel of all four shots using the middle grip, add the follow through. Take an open stance and ask your partner to toss the ball to you. Make contact with the ball outside and in front of your right leg and then pause. Now continue the movement in slow motion, bringing the racket upwards and forwards to the follow-through position.

To help you acquire a sense of the timing and rhythm of the follow through, practice it in slow motion, counting to five between the pause and reaching the final follow-through position.

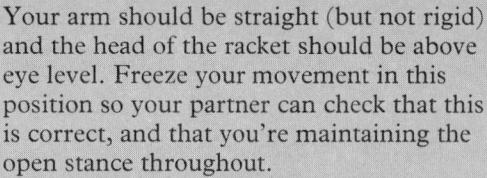

Your arm should be straight (but not rigid) and the head of the racket should be above eye level. Freeze your movement in this position so your partner can check that this is correct, and that you're maintaining the open stance throughout.

As you get the feel of the fluidity of the movement, leave out the pause and combine contact and follow through in one complete action.

MIDDLE GRIP

For the backhand, hold the racket in the backhand middle grip. Get your partner to toss a ball, make contact, pause, and then follow through in slow motion (the slow count to five will help you).

Once again, as you begin to get the feel of the stroke, speed up your movements and follow through from the contact point to the final position without pausing. Your partner should check everything you do.

Try to think of the follow through as helping guide the ball back to your partner. Since the ball stays in contact with the strings longer it will give added control to your shot.

MIDDLE GRIP

Because the volley is a punching or pushing movement from the shoulder, it has very little follow through. You should still practise it with the middle grip, however.

Your partner uses the face of the racket as a target. The contact point is exactly the same for the short grip, with the racket head at eye level, outside and in front of your right shoulder.

Keep the racket face open, so the ball goes back accurately to your partner in a good, high arc. Keep a firm grip so the racket doesn't move when you make contact.

The volley can be an aggressive, attacking shot. Here, though, your concern is simply to practise and you should play the ball gently back to your partner. Take your time getting the feel of the stroke, and exercise firm control to gain the maximum accuracy.

Keep your knees bent so you can adjust your body to the height of the ball, rather than moving your racket. Remember to keep your racket head at eye level. At this stage, of course, your partner should be setting the ball up with sufficient accuracy for you not to have to move to play the volley, but it will be useful practice for later if you take the odd stray ball rather than wasting it.

MIDDLE GRIP

Now rally adding the follow through. Begin with a forehand-to-forehand rally in the middle grip. Because the follow through will give extra length to your shots, you will have to stand further apart. As before, hit the ball more upwards than forwards, to give sufficient time for your partner to react, for you to complete the follow through, and prepare for your next stroke.

Now switch to a backhand-to-backhand rally. While concentrating on the follow through, don't forget what you've already learned: maintain an open stance, keep your eye on the ball the whole time, make contact with it just after it's reached the top of the bounce, and play it back so that it bounces in front of your partner. Above all, exercise firm control over everything you do.

MIDDLE GRIP

While rallying with a forehand to a fore-hand volley, try to picture your follow through guiding the ball on to the target of your partner's racket.

If the ground-stroke player hits the ball too hard, it's the volleyer's responsibility to regain control of the rally by taking the speed off the ball. To do this he takes the racket back slightly on contact, so that it soaks up some of the oncoming ball's momentum, and returns it at a more manageable speed.

MIDDLE GRIP

Before moving on to add the backswing to the shots you've learned, you should change to the full grip.

From the middle grip, simply slide the palm of your hand down so the whole of your hand is holding the grip.

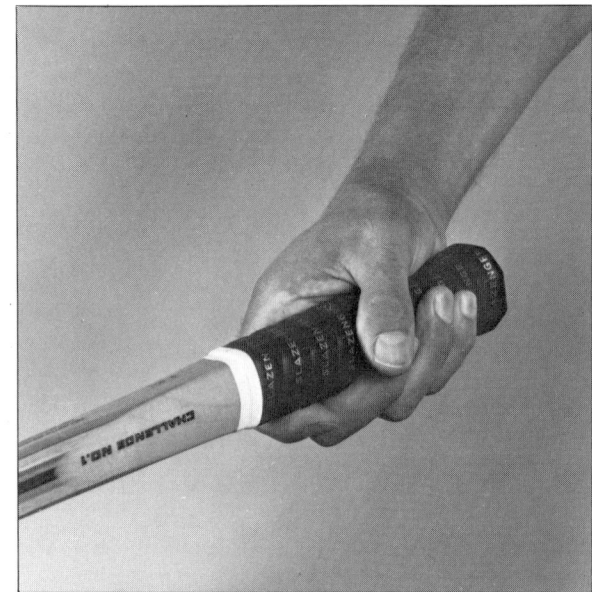

To help you find the grips for the other shots a useful guide is to put a pencil between the upper part of your forefinger and the grip.

On the forehand, adjust your grip so that the pencil is parallel to the face of the racket. When you remove the pencil, the forefinger should stay where it is, so it resembles a trigger finger.

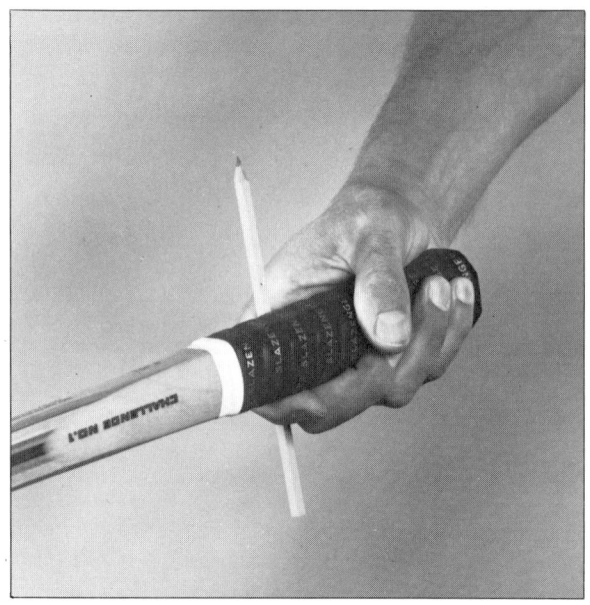

FULL GRIP

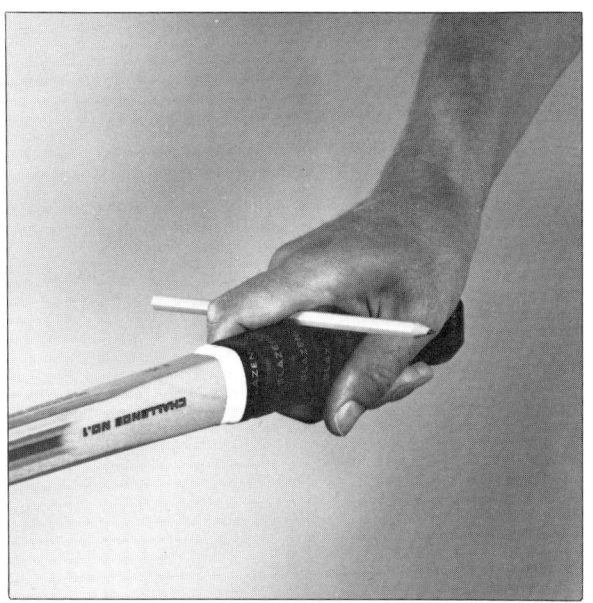

On the backhand, the pencil should be held by the forefinger so that it's at right angles to the face of the racket. After you remove the pencil, keep your finger in this position while playing the shot.

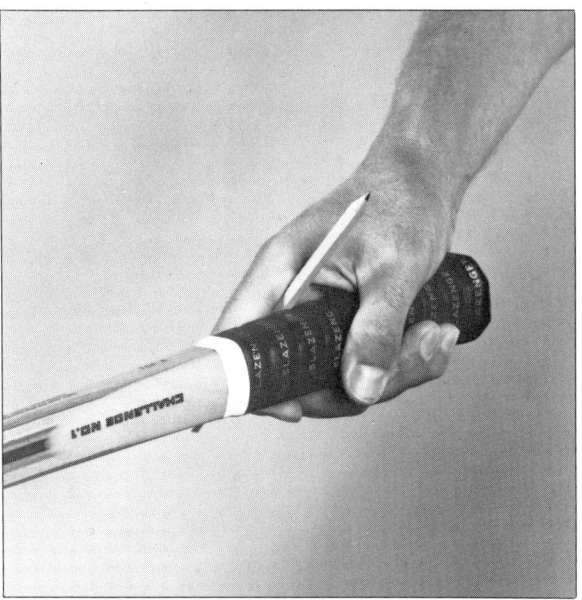

A different grip is used when serving. This service grip is mid-way between the forehand and the backhand grip, so that the pencil will be angled at about 45° to the face of the racket. I will look at this grip more closely in the service section.

These demonstrations with the pencil are intended to show you the essential differences between the grips. You don't need to follow them slavishly: just bear in mind the principle behind each, and adjust your grip so that you can hold the racket comfortably. There will obviously be slight variations for each player.

FULL GRIP

Once you've found a comfortable and effective full grip you can add the backswing to your strokes.

Hold your racket so that, seen from the side, the shaft is parallel to the ground and the frame is on edge.

From the front, your shoulders are slightly turned, with your right elbow close in to your body and your right arm relatively straight and relaxed, as you hold the racket behind you.

As it's difficult for you to look behind to see if you're holding the racket correctly, your partner will have to check from both angles to see that you're doing things right.

FULL GRIP

Starting from this backswing position, ask your partner to toss the ball. Bring the racket forward to make contact with the ball, and then follow through in one easy flowing movement.

Once you can play this shot comfortably from the backswing position, start with the racket at the contact point. Take the racket back at the speed of the oncoming ball to the backswing position. Then bring the racket forward, make contact outside and in front of your right leg, and follow through.

Hold the final follow-through position so your partner can check that your arm is relatively straight, and that the racket head has ended up at just above eye level.

Remember that, now you're using the full grip, the contact point will be further away than previously.

To add fluency to your backswing, start with your racket held head high and your elbow quite close in to your body. Your forearm must be parallel to the ground. Twist your body slightly from the hips, so that your right shoulder is behind the left.

Now bring the racket downwards and behind you in a shallow loop, so that the racket passes through the backswing position, with the frame edge-on to the ground. Your shoulders will turn even more and your arm will straighten.

FULL GRIP

Swing the racket towards the approaching ball and make contact. The movement from the starting position, backwards through the loop and fowards to the contact point, should be continuous.

Maintain your momentum through the point of contact and into the follow through. After a little practice you'll find the whole action, from starting position to the final follow-through position, will become one smooth, continuous swing.

Before trying a rally, get your partner to move you around. Use small, dance-like steps, maintaining an open stance.

On the backhand, keep the shaft parallel to the ground and the racket frame on edge. The right hand rests against your left hip, while your left hand holds the shaft just above the grip.

The shoulders are turned further than on the forehand, because your racket arm has to come across the front of your body.

As before, your partner will need to check that everything is in order before he introduces the ball.

As the ball approaches, swing forward to meet it, your left hand helping to guide the racket towards the ball. Just before you make contact, let go with the left hand.

Swing smoothly into the final follow-through position, with the racket ending up head high. Your arm should be relatively straight but relaxed.

FULL GRIP

To put a loop into the backswing, start with the racket at shoulder height, and take it back to the backswing position. If you have both hands on the racket, you will gain more control over the racket head.

As you move the racket back into the backswing position, try to get the feeling of pulling your right hand on to your left hip. Bring the racket head back at the same height as your left elbow. Pulling the racket back with your left hand as well will help you with this. Take your racket back at the speed of the oncoming ball, and then bring it forward into the stroke in one continuous flowing movement.

FULL GRIP

Make contact with the ball with an open racket face, outside and in front of your left leg, just after the ball has reached the top of the bounce. Play the ball more upwards than forwards so that it goes slowly back to your partner. Then follow through in the usual way.

When you are satisfied that you have mastered this with your partner tossing the ball for you, try using it in a rally. You will have to stand further apart to allow for the extra time the stroke now takes. Despite the fact that the backswing will allow you to add more power to the shot, you should still try to place the ball where your partner can reach it easily. Don't put him under any pressure.

FULL GRIP

There is very little backswing to the volley, but it's well worth practising this stroke with the full grip.

Make contact with the ball playing it upwards and forwards with sufficient control for it to bounce in front of your partner.

Keep the racket at eye level in the full grip, and adjust to any variations in the height of the oncoming ball by flexing your knees.

On the backhand volley, keep your wrist firm to stop the racket moving, and push at the ball with your racket, keeping it square on to your partner.

Keep your feet in an open stance throughout the shot, even though you turn your shoulders and hips.

Once you have mastered the volley with the full grip, you should be able to play any combination of shots using this grip. Try playing a series of rallies.

So far you've always known in advance what shot you're going to play at any given time. You have been able to assume the appropriate starting position from which to play it. From now on, however, you'll be starting off from a neutral or ready position, from which you can move very rapidly to play any of the shots you've learned.

In the ready position your feet are shoulder width apart, with your elbows close in to your body. Hold the racket in front of you with a forehand full grip, while your left hand supports the throat of the racket.

Before your partner introduces the ball, he should tell you to turn. To play a forehand, turn your shoulders to the right to bring the racket round and transfer your weight on to your right leg. Don't move your right arm to bring the racket round; do this by turning your shoulders. When you're in this position your partner can introduce the ball.

THE FOREHAND

As the ball approaches, step forward with the left foot. Take your arm back in a smooth looped backswing and bring the racket forward to make contact with the ball just after the top of the bounce, transferring your full weight on to your left leg as you do so.

As you follow through, pivot from the hips, rotating your shoulders to the left. Keep your weight on the left foot, with the toes of your right foot just touching the ground. Hold the final follow-through position so your partner can see if you're doing it correctly.

You move into the backhand from the same ready position as for the forehand. Start with a forehand grip, but as your shoulders begin to turn to the left, slide your left hand down the racket and change to a backhand grip.

As you move your shoulders, transfer your weight on to your left leg, with the toes of your right foot just touching the ground. The racket moves into the backswing position with both hands pulling it on to the left hip. Your partner can now introduce the ball.

THE BACKHAND

48

As the ball approaches, step in with your right leg and swing the racket forward to make contact.

With your weight still on your right leg, follow through. Notice that, in the backhand follow through, the shoulders are side-on to your partner, in contrast to the more open position on the forehand.

The forehand volley starts once again from the ready position.

When your partner tells you to turn, move your shoulders round to bring the racket into the contact position and transfer your weight on to your right leg. He can now toss the ball to you, using your racket as a target.

THE FOREHAND VOLLEY

Just before you make contact with the ball, step firmly on to your left leg, leaving the toes of your right foot just touching the ground. Contact should be made with the ball at eye level, with the elbow relatively close to the body. Holding your left hand out in front of you will help you judge the speed and distance of the approaching ball.

There is very little follow through with the volley. Simply bring your shoulders round to a more open position. Your weight should still be on your left leg.

Take up the ready position again for the backhand volley. Turn and slide your left hand down the racket, changing to a backhand grip.

Transfer your weight on to your left leg with your right shoulder facing your partner. Your left hand should hold the racket just above the grip to help you control the racket head. Your partner can now introduce the ball.

THE BACKHAND VOLLEY

Just before you make contact, let go with the left hand and step on to your right foot, transferring your weight as you do so.

Because the volley is a push or a punch, there is very little follow through. Note that, on the backhand, the shoulders are more closed than on the forehand.

Before you start the rally, it's essential to learn how to set the ball up for yourself from the ready position. Turn your shoulders and take the racket back. Toss the ball up, so it will bounce to the correct height and distance for you to make good contact just after the top of the bounce.

As the ball bounces, step in with your left foot, make contact and follow through.

INTRODUCING THE BALL

To set the ball up for the backhand, the left hand, holding the ball, must go over the racket as you bring the latter back.

Toss the ball up and step in with the right foot. Make contact just after the top of the bounce and follow through.

It is important to get this first ball of a rally absolutely right, so your partner can play it easily on the return.

All the shots you've learned so far have involved only very simple footwork. Now you'll learn more foot movements, to get you from the ready position into the position where you will play your shot.

Take up the ready position, turn, and ask your partner to toss the ball to your right so that you will have to run a short distance to play your forehand.

As you turn towards the ball, your weight will be on your right foot, so it will be easier to make your first step with your left. Run in this position with your racket held high and your left shoulder facing towards your partner.

THE FOREHAND

You play the forehand with your weight on the left leg, so judge your steps in order to arrive in the correct position, with your left leg leading.

Make contact and follow through. Hold the final position so your partner can check that all is as it should be.

From the illustrations you can see how the three steps have been made from the ready position. The player starts with his left leg, then takes another step with his right, and a final one with the left to get into position. The number of steps you take depends on how far you have to move, but the important point to remember at first in playing the forehand is to start and finish with the left foot.

To play the backhand, stand in the ready position and have your partner toss the ball to your left.

Turn to your left into the backswing position. Initially your weight will be on your left foot so it will be easier to move off with your right.

THE BACKHAND

Run in this backswing position, gauging your steps so you will arrive to play the ball with your weight on your right foot.

Again, the number of steps you take will be relative to the distance you have to cover, but on the backhand it will help you at first to start and finish on your right foot. After completing the stroke, side-step back to the original position.

If a ball comes straight at you, you'll have to move away from it to play a forehand. Get your partner to toss the ball directly towards you. It should bounce slightly short so you'll have to move sideways around the ball.

Such steps are more of a sideways dance than a run, particularly since you are moving away from the ball. On the forehand move off with the left foot.

THE FOREHAND

The space you've created by moving away from the ball allows you to step in with your left leg and make contact. The footprints in the illustration show how you dance around the ball.

The skill in this type of shot lies in being far enough away from the bouncing ball, to be able to step in and make contact correctly without being cramped.

FULL GRIP

61

You may, of course, want to take the ball coming directly at you on the backhand rather than the forehand. Move quickly into the turned position with your weight on the left leg.

Step off with your right foot, and create space by moving away from the line of the oncoming ball. This will allow you to step in with your right foot and make contact. Hold the racket in the backswing position as you move.

THE BACKHAND

Before you swing the racket forward to make contact, step towards the ball with your right leg, and transfer your weight on to this foot.

With the backhand, it's helpful at first to begin and end on your right foot. The quicker you can move into position, the more time you will have to play your shot and exercise control over the ball.

Volleys are very much reaction shots, since you rarely have much time to play them.

For a forehand volley start in the ready position, turn and ask your partner to introduce the ball to your right. Step in with the left foot and make contact.

To play a ball coming straight at you, however, sway to the left out of its way, to give yourself room to make your stroke.

FOREHAND VOLLEYS

If the ball is too far away for you to reach with one step, side-step towards it, and then step in with your left foot to make contact.

Practise playing the short ball, tossed by your partner, by turning and stepping directly towards the ball to take it early.

Use similar footwork on the backhand. From the ready position, reach a ball tossed to your left by stepping across with the right foot.

Sway to your right, on to your right leg, to take the ball tossed directly at you by your partner.

BACKHAND VOLLEYS

Now get your partner to toss the ball so far over to your left that you won't be able to reach it with a single step. Cover the extra distance by side-stepping to your left. Then step across and forward with the right leg to make contact.

For the ball tossed short, step well forward towards it and make contact early. While you're concentrating on improving your mobility in playing the volley, don't forget that the stroke is a punching movement from the shoulder.

These are the basic variations of moving to play the volley. You should adapt your footwork to play the ball in different subtler situations.

You will often see players bobbing up and down in an open stance when they're in the ready position. This is called a split step.

These jumps don't have to be very high – they are merely a way of keeping on your toes so you're ready to move off quickly in any direction.

THE SPLIT STEPS

For instance, on the forehand volley, as the ball approaches transfer your weight to the right leg and turn the shoulders.

You can move quickly into the turned position for the forehand volley using the split step. You'll see it being used most clearly by players about to receive a service or by a volleyer at the net.

The service is the most important shot in any player's game. It's the only shot which enables you to set the ball up exactly where you want it, and to take your time about playing your stroke.

Played correctly, it will enable you to gain an advantage over your opponent. But you need to exercise great control over your service, because when you serve, you have to hit the ball into a smaller area ie the service court.

THE COMPLETE STROKE

I've treated the service separately in this book, not because it's any more difficult than the other shots, but because, although the method is the same, the procedure for learning it is slightly different.

I suggest you start without a racket to give you a sense of the co-ordination of the arm movements. You don't need a partner to practise your service but if there are two of you, you can help correct each other.

THE COMPLETE STROKE

THE SERVICE

Start by establishing the contact point. Stretch your right arm high above your head, with the fingers outspread.

Hold the ball palm-up in your fingertips, with your left arm out in front of you so it is parallel to the ground. Your weight should be firmly anchored on your left leg.

Bring your left hand down and then up, releasing the ball into the air so it will travel straight up into your right hand. This will establish the contact point.

Practise tossing the ball up so you can place it accurately into your right hand without having to move your right arm.

BY HAND

When you're able to do this easily, you should add the follow through. Having caught the ball in the contact position with your right arm outstretched, bring the arm forward and downwards, turning your hand so the palm faces to your right. Do this in slow motion at first.

Continue bringing your arm down so the final position for the follow through will be with your right arm between your left arm and your body.

Repeat the exercise, catching the ball at the contact point but this time, instead of holding your right hand in the air in the contact position, start with it behind your head. Hold your left arm out in front of you as before and place the ball into the air.

Just before the ball reaches the top of its flight, bring your right hand out from behind your head and catch the ball. This will give you the feel of the throwing action which characterises the service. Once you're used to this throwing action, you can add the follow through.

BY HAND

To get a feeling of the co-ordinated rhythm of the service, both arms must work together. Start with both arms held in front of the body – the ready position for the service – with the ball in your left hand. Now take both arms down together, the left arm to the left thigh, the right arm back behind your body. As you do so, your weight should be on your back (right) foot.

Then bring both arms up together. The right arm goes up until it stretches out horizontally behind you. The left comes up in front of you and releases the ball into the air as before. Don't bring your right hand forward to catch it, however, catch the ball again in your left hand at the highest point.

Now you can combine these two exercises. Start in the ready position with both arms forward, and take them down together.

Bring the arms up, place the ball into the air and this time bring your right arm back, bending the elbow, so you can tap the back of your head twice.

The second tap should be just before you catch the ball with your left hand. Practise doing this until the timing and rhythm come naturally.

Then repeat the exercise, tapping the back of the head once but, instead of tapping it a second time, bring your arm forward in a throwing motion to catch the ball at the contact point in your right hand.

Practise this until you have co-ordinated the full service action, and feel ready to use a racket.

Now you can start to use a racket. You've already seen how to hold it in the service grip, using a pencil as a guide. Another easy way to find the service grip is by bouncing a ball up and down on the ground using the edge of the racket. To keep control over the ball, you'll have to make a chopping motion with the racket, and the way you'll naturally hold it to do this will be close to the service grip.

Having found a comfortable way of holding the racket in the service grip, stretch out your right arm to hold the racket up in the contact position. Anchor your weight firmly on your left (forward) foot, and place the ball into the air. You will have to toss it a little higher than before to allow for the additional length of the racket. Make contact with the ball by tapping it gently with an open racket face.

FULL GRIP

Once you can toss the ball up to the right height and make contact in the centre of the racket, bring the racket forward and downwards in slow motion. Turn your palm outwards so the racket is on edge throughout the follow through.

Bring your racket down outside your left leg so that it passes between your left arm and your body.

Always place the ball accurately into the air so that, at this stage, you don't have to move your feet to chase it.

Next start by holding the racket behind you, with the head of the racket down between your shoulder blades.

Place the ball into the air, remembering to keep your weight on the back foot.

Bring the racket out from behind your back towards the contact position with a throwing movement, shifting your weight forward on to the front foot as you do so. Make contact with the ball and then stop. You add the follow through once you can make contact with the ball consistently and accurately, and can dispense with the stop.

FULL GRIP

Now get a feel of the rhythm of the whole service from start to finish. Begin by holding both arms out in front of you with the racket edge-on to the ground, in the ready position for the service. Your weight is on your back foot.

Take the arms down together, just as before, and bring them up again to their respective positions: racket arm coming up horizontally behind you, left hand releasing the ball and then catching it again at the highest possible point.

Once you've got the timing for the swing of the arms right, you can try the double-tap exercise with the racket behind your back. Start from the ready position.

Bring the arms down together and up again as before, but this time continue the movement of the racket until it's straight out behind you at the moment you release the ball. Continue on, to tap your back twice with the edge of your racket, so that you're catching the ball with your left hand just after the second tap.

When you've got the timing right between catching and tapping, replace the second tap with the throwing action of the racket out to the contact point. Make contact and then pause.

FULL GRIP

Having made contact with the ball correctly, add the follow through. As the service becomes more natural to you, you should leave out the stop and make it one continuous movement from start to finish. The pace of the first part of the movement – taking the arms down and then back again – should be slow and assured. Power for the service is generated when you pick up speed by throwing the racket head at the ball from behind your back.

I've deliberately shown you how to serve without moving your feet. Having learned from the start how to place the ball accurately into the air, you won't have needed to move in order to reach it. Now, having established a rhythmic, co-ordinated serve, bring your right foot over the baseline after making contact. Make it as positive, forceful step as you follow through. This will provide power for your shot and, equally importantly, will get you into motion ready to take your partner's return.

DRILLS

Player **A** serves onto player **B**'s forehand. **B** should trap the ball on the racket strings to check good contact (see p. 90). Then repeat the drill with **B** serving to **A**. For every successful service take a pace back. Continue until you are serving with accuracy and control from the baseline.

A serves onto **B**'s backhand and **B** returns the service. After each successful service both take a step backwards. When **A** is serving successfully from the baseline – stop – and repeat the drill with **B** serving.

1

2

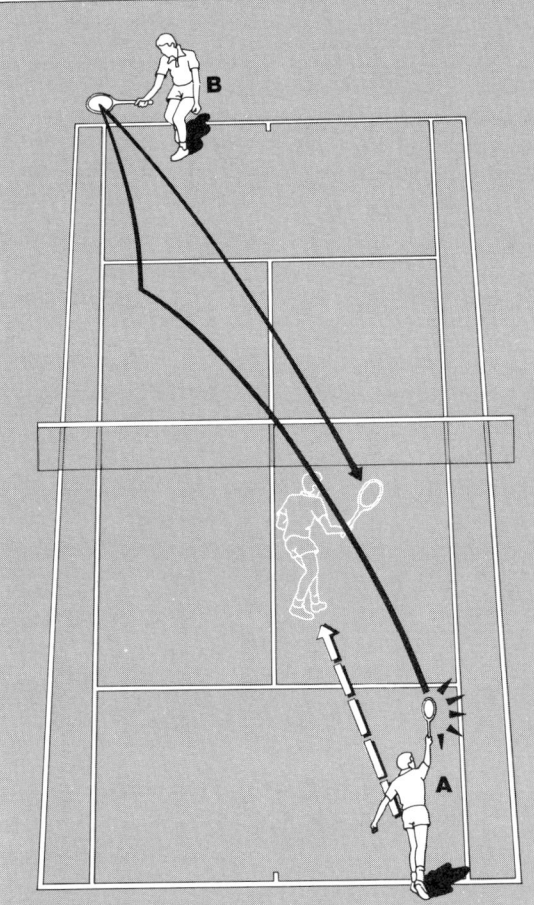

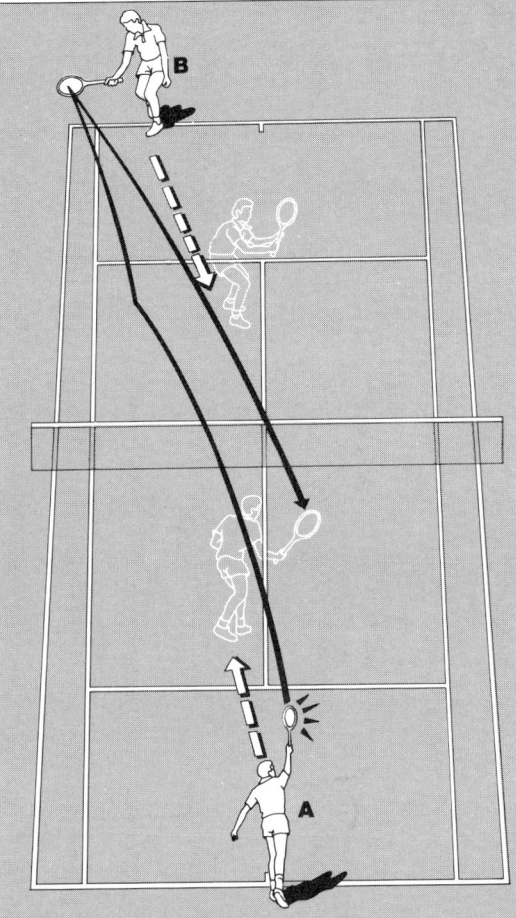

A serves from the baseline onto B's forehand and advances to the net. B plays a controlled forehand for A to play a forehand volley. Continue the rally until it breaks down then repeat with B serving. This drill can also be played on the backhand side.

A serves from the baseline onto B's forehand and advances to the net. B plays a controlled forehand for A to volley. B then also advances to the net and starts a volley to volley rally. Repeat the drill with B serving. This drill can also be played on the backhand side.

The drills that follow are for 3 or 4 people. **A** and **B**, playing forehands, maintain an easy rhythmic rally. On every second ball from **A**, **C** intercepts with a controlled forehand volley enabling **A** to play it to **B** again. After a few successful rallies change positions.

The same drill can be practised on the backhand. **A** and **B** play a backhand rally and **C** intercepts every second ball from **A** with a backhand volley and returns to the ready position. It's **C**'s responsibility in these drills to take the speed off the ball if it's being played too hard.

5

6

This drill is a development of the two previous drills. **A** and **B** play a groundstroke rally. **C** intercepts with a forehand volley and continues to the other side of the court.

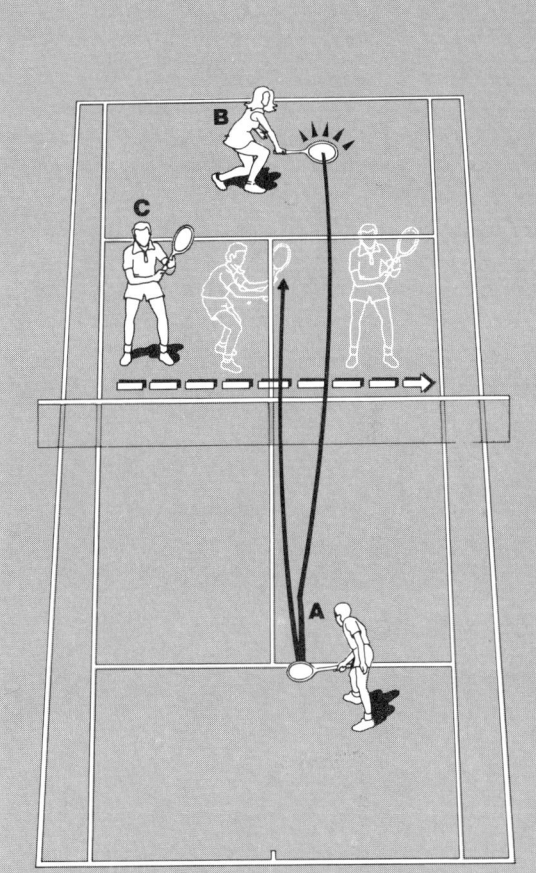

Now **C** intercepts with a backhand volley as he continues back to his starting position. It's important to play these drills with control at first. As you improve you can increase the distance of your groundstrokes from the net while adding more power to your shots.

7

8

A serves over the net to **B**. **B** plays a forehand to **C** who volleys to **D**. **D** volleys the ball back to bounce in front of **A** who starts the cycle again with a forehand.

This is the same as the previous drill except that once **B** has played his first shot he approaches the net. On the next cycle **B** will play a volley.

9

10

This is also a development of the previous drill. This time **A** also advances to the net after his first shot and all four players end up volleying at the net. Change positions every so often so that all four players get practice in coming to the net.

This drill is for 3 players. **A** plays to **B**'s forehand volley. On the return **A** then plays to **C**'s forehand volley. **A** then plays to **C**'s backhand volley and the cycle starts again. This drill allows **C**, who doesn't see the ball until almost too late, to improve his reactions.

11

12

Even at this stage, when I've shown you all the basic shots and footwork involved in tennis and you've been able to put them into a rally with your partner, it's quite possible that you might be overlooking one or two small points which could affect your game. From my own experience of teaching beginners, I'd suggest faults might lie within the following areas.

For instance, you may not be making contact right in the centre of the racket. Try trapping a ball tossed by your partner against the strings with your left hand the instant you make contact.

If the ball isn't in the centre of the strings, place it there with your left hand. Then get your partner to set the ball up once more, and try again. Carry on doing this until you can smother the ball with your left hand in the centre. You can try this exercise with any of the grips, from short to full.

HINTS & IDEAS

If you find that you're putting too much backswing into your volley (your partner will tell you if you are), try tying a piece of string between the racket and the net, and pull it taut. You'll find this will force you to push forward at the ball, because it prevents you from moving the racket back.

If you're letting the racket head drop midway though your ground strokes, stand in the contact position with your racket edge-on and parallel to the ground. Now have your partner tie a piece of string tautly between your elbow and the racket head. Practise making strokes with the string in position, to show you how the angle of the wrist should remain constant.

VISUAL AIDS

If you can't keep your racket firm while volleying, try holding it with both hands on the shoulders of the racket head, looking directly through the strings at the ball. As you push at the oncoming ball, you'll get a sense of firmness about the pushing movement, and this is what you should try to reproduce in the one-handed volleys.

If you find that you're moving your racket arm too far away from your body on the backswing, you can rectify this by putting a ball under your armpit. You'll have to pull your arm in close to keep the ball there during the backswing. As you pass through the contact point the ball will drop away naturally. This is how your arm should be during the normal exercise.

HINTS & IDEAS

If your partner tells you your racket isn't on edge during the backswing, crouch down and tap the ground behind you with the racket. You'll soon be able to tell if the racket is on edge or not.

If you're not following through correctly, stand with your back to a wall (about $1-1\frac{1}{2}$ ft away for the forehand, closer in for the backhand) and your feet together. Your partner should toss the ball parallel to the wall, so that it bounces in front of you. Step sideways towards the oncoming ball, play your backhand or forehand and then follow through. In the final follow-through position, your racket head should be just touching the wall.

THE RACKET

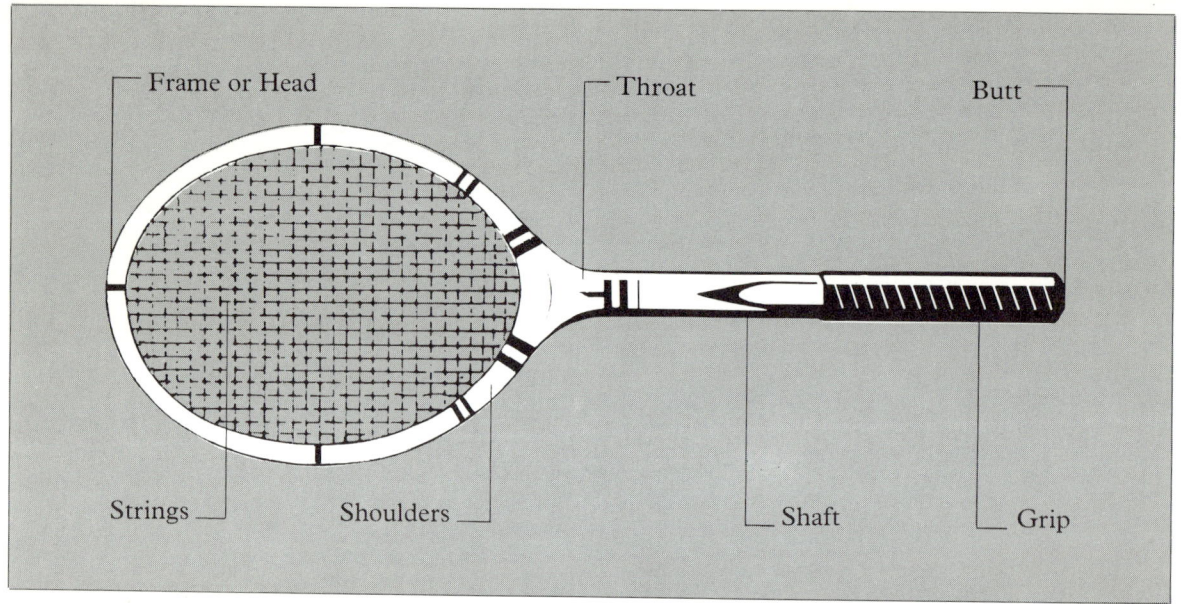

Frame or Head — Throat — Butt

Strings — Shoulders — Shaft — Grip

Doubles side line	◄ Net	
Service Line ►	Left hand service court	Right hand service court
◄ Baseline	Right hand service court	Left hand service court
▲ Singles side line	◄ Net	

Centre mark ►

THE COURT

SIMPLIFIED RULES

Tennis is a game for two or four players.

1 Begin by ensuring the top of the net is three feet from the ground at its centre.

2 Toss a coin or spin a racket to decide who serves first or who has choice of ends.

3 Each point must be started by serving from alternate sides of the centre mark, behind the baseline, the first service from the right hand side.

4 You may have two attempts at serving.

5 While serving, a *Fault* is called when:

a) You don't get the ball to bounce into your opponents service court;
b) You swing at the ball and miss;
c) The ball goes into the net;
d) You step on or over the baseline with either foot before hitting the ball.

6 You may also receive a *Let*. A let means the service should be retaken because:

a) The ball hits the top of the net and still goes into your opponents service court;
b) You hit the ball into your opponents service court before they're ready to receive;
c) You toss the ball and catch it again without attempting to strike it.

7 Your opponent can stand in any position he chooses to receive serve but must not volley the ball back, it must bounce first.

8 You can lose a point by:
a) Letting the ball bounce twice;
b) Your racket or clothing touching the net;
c) The ball touching your clothing;
d) Playing the ball before it passes over the net;
e) Letting go of the racket, even if it hits the ball.

9 Shots are good if they hit the line, or hit the net and go over (apart from the service).

10 Tennis has its own scoring system.

Love   = 0
1st score = 15
2nd score = 30
3rd score = 40
4th score = Game

The server's score is always given first. Here is an example:

You (the server) win 1st point 15–Love.
Your opponent wins 2nd point 15–15.
Your opponent wins 3rd point 15–30.
You win 4th point 30–30.
You win 5th point 40–30.
If your opponent wins 6th point you do not say 40–40 you use another word *Deuce*.
After Deuce you must win 2 points in succession to win the game.
The first of these 2 points is called *Advantage In* if the server wins it, and *Advantage Out* if the opponent wins it.
If you have the Advantage and win the next point, you win the game, if your opponent wins you return to Deuce.

For a *Match* you add the *Games* up into what are called *Sets*.
You win a Set if you win 6 Games with at least a 2 Game advantage, for example: 6–0; 6–1; 6–2; 6–3; 6–4 but you cannot win a Set 6–5 because there is only 1 Game advantage, it must be 7–5.

To win a Match you must win the best of 3 or 5 Sets depending on what you and your opponent have pre-arranged.

More detailed rules can be found in 'The International Tennis Federation Rule Book'.

INDEX